This book belongs to:

Brady

Sienna

LUCY COOKE

a little
book of
SLOTH

Margaret K. McElderry Books
New York • London • Toronto • Sydney • New Delhi • Slothville

I love sloths. I always have. I love their sweet smiles, slo-mo lifestyle, and innate hugability. I believe that being fast is overrated and that the sloth is the true king of the jungle. But he's rarely seen as such, so I founded the Sloth Appreciation Society, of which you are now a member.

In a sleepy corner of Costa Rica there's an upside-down world where sloth is a virtue and not a sin. A sanctuary—the first in the world—devoted to saving this much maligned animal.

Home to one hundred and fifty orphaned and injured sloths, Slothville is an idle idyll where the sloths' every whim is catered for by the celebrated sloth whisperer Judy Arroyo.

This book reveals some of the secrets behind the sloth's smile and introduces you to a handful of the sanctuary's superstar sloths. I think we have much to learn from their mellow ways. So take a break from the hectic world around you, kick back, relax, and enjoy hanging with the sloths.

Lucy Cooke

It all started with Buttercup.

Baby Buttercup turned up on Judy's doorstep
as a tiny orphan. She was a few weeks old
and desperately needed a new mom.

Buttercup's new home offered more
slouching opportunities than your average
tree branch. So she chose the best seat in
the house and decided to stay.

Two decades later she's still there. Buttercup is the queen of Slothville. She rules over her slumbering empire from her very own wicker throne. As a wise and benevolent leader, her sole decree is that everyone just chill.

Word got out that there was a place that cared for sloths in need . . .

. . . and soon sloths
were everywhere.

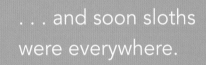

The burgeoning brood brought together two families of sloth. They are defined by how many digits they have. But you don't have to count their fingers to tell them apart. On Buttercup's side, the *Bradypus*, or three-fingered sloth, is the Muppet with the medieval haircut and Mona Lisa smile.

The *Choloepus* are
cousins of the
Bradypus and have
just two fingers.
They look more like a
cross between a Wookie
and a pig.

All sloths, like little baby Velcro, love to hang out.

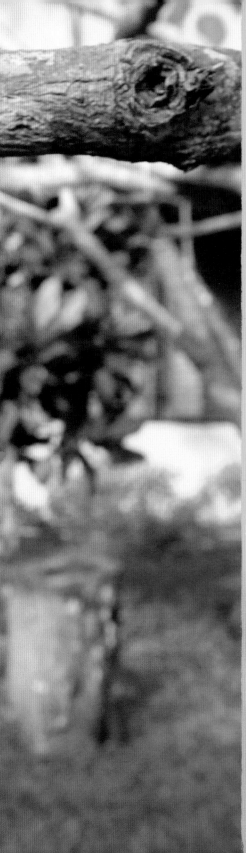

Sloths' natural home is the jungles of South and Central America where they spend their whole lives hanging about in trees. Literally. Their long arms and curved claws help them hook on and hang around without spending much energy, allowing for optimum laziness. Sixty million years of evolution have made sloths the absolute masters of mellow.

Not only do sloths spend 70 percent of their time, *ahem*, "resting," but their nerves may even have evolved to not react to loud noises. So there's no point saying *BOO!* to a sloth. They are simply too chilled out to notice.

Sloths aren't monkeys or bears but Xenarthrans, which makes them sound like they are from outer space, and they have a sci-fi biology to match. For a start, sloths can't control body temperature like other mammals, so they bask in the sun like reptiles to warm up in the morning. The nights can be a trifle chilly for a baby sloth who no longer has his mom to cling to. So Judy invented specialized sloth onesies for those in extreme need.

A sloth can't pop down to the shops and buy these. They are hand-crafted from old sports socks.

Here's hoping they remembered to wash them first.

Baby sloths are Jedi masters of the hug. Their innate hugability helps them cling to their moms for the first year of their lives.

They love to hug so much; collectively, they form a *cuddle puddle*.

It's important that a baby sloth find just the right snuggle partner, so the orphaned babies get stuffies to hug in place of their moms.

Mateo was especially fussy with his choice.
He tried quite a few before deciding on . . .

. . . Mr. Moo.

Mateo is so cute, he
should come with a
public health warning.

But don't be fooled by his sweetie-pie looks. This sloth has attitude. Mateo's a streetwise sloth who was found abandoned near the capital city. He's a bit of a loner and prefers the soft but silent company of Moo to hanging out with the other sloths. If any of the other baby sloths tries to sneak a Moo hug, a fight breaks out—a very, very slow fight, in which the winner is the last sloth to stay awake.

Wild sloths are solitary animals, but the sanctuary sloths make friends for life. Sunshine and Sammy were rescued from poachers who wanted to sell them as pets. They arrived within days of each other and have been on a hugging marathon ever since. Their party trick is this impersonation of a freaky double-headed sloth monster. It makes people squeal—but from cute overload, not fear. Just don't tell Sunshine and Sammy that.

If hugging were an Olympic sport, then Ubu would be a gold medalist, but he wasn't always so strong. As a baby, Ubu lost his grip on his mother and fell. When he hit the ground he hurt his spine, and now his back legs don't work. But plenty of physical therapy has given this paraplegic baby sloth the upper body strength of a champion wrestler. He'll never let go of another sloth again. Even Mateo, who only tolerates Ubu's monster hugs by dreaming of Moo.

Ubu's not the only sloth to require special medical treatment. Orphan babies often arrive with broken bones and other mysterious problems. The sanctuary has its very own "slothpital" to treat sloths with special needs.

Some sloths are more special than others, like the twins Violet and Sebastian.

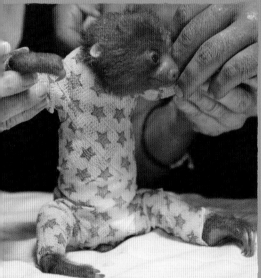

Their trip to the slothpital resulted in a serious fashion overhaul. Out went the old sock pajamas and in came some seriously snazzy bandages. Although Violet was somewhat jealous that her brother got the blue stars, and Sebastian felt that pink was much more his color.

Did somebody order a bucket of sloth? Every home should have one: a party-size bucket with plenty of sloth hugs to go around. Bucket, by the way, is the sloths' favorite way to travel. It's fast. It's like flying. And it allows them to snooze on the move. Sweet.

What sloths lack in speed they make up for in fancy arboreal acrobatics. Three-fingered sloths are the only mammal on the planet with extra neck vertebrae and can turn their heads up to 270 degrees. So even when they are upside down, their smiles are the right way up.

There's no time to be a slouch at the sanctuary. All baby sloths have a daily workout on the jungle gym to polish their climbing skills.

Work it, Wally! Wally is a hard-working young sloth, dedicated to self-improvement. He has finally learned how to climb up. But he's yet to master the art of reverse and often has to be rescued from the top.

At the sanctuary the sloths take a regular splash in a special green leaf tea to keep their skin healthy.

Wild sloths are actually green. Their coats are mini jungles of algae and insects, including a moth that only lives on a sloth. They look and smell just like trees. Sloths are like stealth ninjas, and these invisible cloaks prevent them from becoming eagle food. Which is just as well. Since their top speed is fifteen feet a minute, running from danger is simply not an option.

When their beauty treatment finishes, the baby sloths are hung out to dry. Of course, with sloths there's no need for clothespins.

After his trip to the sloth salon, Mateo looks even more like a puffball, which kind of annoys him. But he's finally reunited with Moo again. *Phew.*

It has to be said that sloths have very poor table manners. They *nom nom* with their mouths open and frequently fall asleep in their food.

But not Honey. She is a terribly refined sloth with manners straight out of a Swiss sloth finishing school. Here you see her demonstrating the correct way to hold a bean. Who knew a sloth could be so posh?

Sloths love beans, but they go nuts for hibiscus flowers. Hibiscus flowers are like sloth chocolate. But without the calories.

Some sloths gobble the flowers up straightaway. Others, like Velcro, prefer to hold off and savor the moment before finally giving in.

With his fabulous Buddha belly, Biscuit, like all sloths, is a bit on the portly side. But in his own way Biscuit is an athlete. A digesting athlete.

A sloth's diet is the key to its slothfulness. In the wild, sloths don't eat beans like the sloths at the sanctuary eat. Their diet consists of jungle leaves that are a bit toxic and don't provide much energy. Their secret weapon is a big tummy like Biscuit's and lots of time. It takes them four weeks to digest one meal and their stomach contents make up two thirds of their body weight. They need to take it easy or they'd suffer terrible indigestion.

To potty train a baby
sloth you will need:

1 baby sloth

1 poo pole

quite a lot
of patience

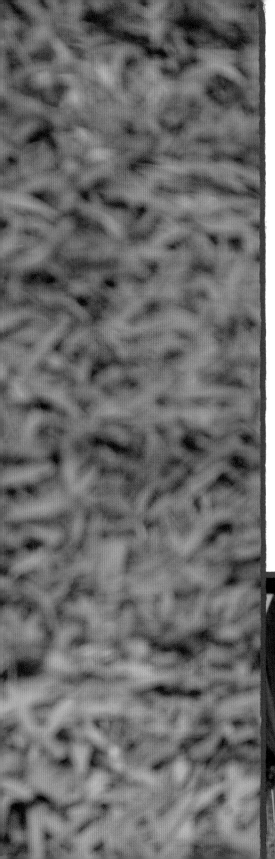

Wild sloths have somewhat bizarre bathroom habits. Once a week they descend from the safety of their treetop homes to do their business at the base of a tree. Such eccentric etiquette is one of the great mysteries of sloth behavior.

The sanctuary sloths must learn to do the same. Just don't hurry them. Sloths, after all, hate to be hurried, especially while on the job. Although some, like Cosmo, get a bit confused about the point of the poo pole.

No one knows how long a sloth can live. But Queen Buttercup has just turned twenty, making her the oldest living captive three-fingered sloth. She's celebrating with a sloth's favorite kind of party: a slumber party.

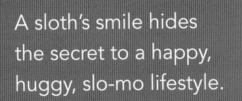

A sloth's smile hides the secret to a happy, huggy, slo-mo lifestyle.

Take a cue from nature's couch potato and heed
Queen Buttercup's decree:

just
chill.

Slothville Yearbook

Violet and Sebastian: Slothville's resident fashionistas; often seen modeling next season's attire.

Wally: Dreams of setting a world record for climbing Mount Everest. Slowly.

Buttercup: The Queen of Sloth throws the best sort of fest—a snooze fest.

Honey: Behind her sweet smile lurks a supersneaky bean thief.

Ubu: The Captain of Cuddles; even practices hugging in his sleep.

Mateo: The Dark Lord of Cute; has the power to paralyze with a single sloth squeak.

Sunshine and Sammy: Maintain the ideal cuddle ratio: one part sleep, two parts arm, and the remaining parts love.

Velcro: Always reaches for the stars. Often falls asleep on the way.

The babies in this book are undeniably cute, but please remember that sloths belong in the wild and should never be kept as pets. If you want to "adopt" a sloth, visit the Aviarios del Caribe sloth sanctuary website (slothsanctuary.com) and make a donation. They won't send you an orphaned sloth, but they will care for it until it can be released back into the wild where it belongs.

To share your sloth love and join the Sloth Appreciation Society, visit slothville.com.

To Martha, Isabel, Stella, Jed, and Samson

MARGARET K. McELDERRY BOOKS
An imprint of Simon & Schuster Children's Publishing Division • 1230 Avenue of the Americas, New York, New York 10020 • Copyright © 2013 by Lucy Cooke • All rights reserved, including the right of reproduction in whole or in part in any form. • MARGARET K. McELDERRY BOOKS is a trademark of Simon & Schuster, Inc. • For information about special discounts for bulk purchases, please contact Simon & Schuster Special Sales at 1-866-506-1949 or business@simonandschuster.com. • The Simon & Schuster Speakers Bureau can bring authors to your live event. For more information or to book an event, contact the Simon & Schuster Speakers Bureau at 1-866-248-3049 or visit our website at www.simonspeakers.com. • Book design by Lauren Rille • The text for this book is set in Avenir. • Manufactured in China • Library of Congress Cataloging-in-Publication Data • Cooke, Lucy, 1970– • A little book of sloth / Lucy Cooke. • p. cm. • ISBN 978-1-4424-4557-4 (hardcover) • ISBN 978-1-4424-4558-1 (eBook) • 1. Sloths—Juvenile literature. 2. Sloths—Costa Rica—Juvenile literature. I. Title. • QL737.E2C66 2013 • 599.3'13—dc23 • 2012018737
0114 SCP
10 9 8 7 6 5 4

Photo credits: Gabriella di Caprio: jacket front flap (center) • © Jenny Jozwiak: pages 26–27 (all); page 28 (top left) • Frank Lang: jacket back panel (center left, bottom center); page 19 • Rebecca Mills: page 12 (bottom left); page 42 (all); page 46 (center) • Philip Stebbing: pages 6–7 • All other photos by Lucy Cooke